Alan Bullard

Wondrous Cross

A meditation based on the traditional 'Seven Last Words' of Jesus Christ

for SATB choir and organ or piano
with optional soloists, congregation, and strings

MUSIC DEPARTMENT

OXFORD
UNIVERSITY PRESS

OXFORD
UNIVERSITY PRESS

Great Clarendon Street, Oxford OX2 6DP, England

Oxford University Press is a department of the University of Oxford.
It furthers the University's aim of excellence in research, scholarship,
and education by publishing worldwide in

Oxford New York

Auckland Bangkok Buenos Aires Cape Town Chennai
Dar es Salaam Delhi Hong Kong Istanbul Karachi Kolkata
Kuala Lumpur Madrid Melbourne Mexico City Mumbai Nairobi
São Paulo Shanghai Taipei Tokyo Toronto

Oxford is a registered trade mark of Oxford University Press
in the UK and in certain other countries

1 3 5 7 9 10 8 6 4 2

ISBN 978-0-19-337989-3

Printed in Great Britain on acid-free paper by
Halstan & Co. Ltd., Amersham, Bucks.

Contents

	Text	4
1.	Prelude	7
2.	The First Words	8
3.	Hymn: There is a green hill far away	9
4.	The Second Words	11
5.	The Third Words	14
6.	Hymn: When my love to God grows weak	16
7.	The Fourth Words	18
8.	Chorus (or solo): Drop, drop, slow tears	19
9.	Chorus/Hymn: Were you there?	22
10.	The Fifth Words	27
11.	Chorus and solo/semi-chorus: Ave verum corpus	28
12.	The Sixth Words	33
13.	Arioso: God so loved the world	33
14.	The Seventh Words	37
15.	Chorus: In the departure of the Lord	37
16.	Hymn: When I survey the Wondrous Cross	38

Instrumentation

The work may be accompanied in two ways:

1. **With organ or piano**, using the keyboard accompaniment printed in the vocal score.

2. **With organ or piano and strings**—string quartet, or quintet, or ensemble. In this version the keyboard player should omit those passages in square brackets in the vocal score. String parts and full scores are available to purchase or hire from the publisher's Hire Library or appropriate agent.

Composer's note

Wondrous Cross is designed for liturgical use or as a concert piece. If performed liturgically, the congregation may join in the three hymns and also the first and last verses of 'Were you there?'. The work may also be interspersed with prayers and readings.

The work is designed with some vocal flexibility in mind, and may be sung entirely by SATB choir, with groups of singers taking the unison lines, or by SATB choir and a range of soloists. Several movements, including the settings of 'Drop, drop, slow tears' and 'Ave verum corpus', may be extracted from the work for separate performance.

Duration: *c*.30 minutes (without any additional prayers or readings).

Text

The text is largely from the Authorized Version of the Bible and focuses on Jesus's 'Seven Last Words'. These are sayings attributed to Jesus on the cross, and are to be found in the four Gospels. Traditionally they are used as a Christian meditation for Lent, Holy Week, and Good Friday.

1. Prelude

2. The First Words

And when they were come to the place, which is called Calvary, there they crucified him and the malefactors, one on the right hand, and the other on the left. Then said Jesus, Father, forgive them; for they know not what they do.

> Luke 23: 33–4

3. Hymn: There is a green hill far away

1. There is a green hill far away,
   Outside a city wall,
   Where the dear Lord was crucified,
   Who died to save us all.

2. We may not know, we cannot tell,
   What pains he had to bear,
   But we believe it was for us
   He hung and suffered there.

3. He died that we might be forgiv'n,
   He died to make us good,
   That we might go at last to heav'n,
   Saved by his precious blood.

4. O dearly, dearly has he loved,
   And we must love him too,
   And trust in his redeeming blood,
   And try his works to do.

> C. F. Alexander

4. The Second Words

And one of the malefactors which were hanged railed on him, saying, If thou be Christ, save thyself and us. But the other answering rebuked him saying, Dost thou not fear God, seeing thou art in the same condemnation? And we indeed justly; for we receive the due reward of our deeds: but this man hath done nothing amiss. And he said unto Jesus, Lord, remember me when thou comest into thy kingdom. And Jesus said unto him, Verily I say unto thee, Today shalt thou be with me in paradise.

> Luke 23: 39–43

5. The Third Words

Now there stood by the cross of Jesus his mother, and his mother's sister, Mary the wife of Cleophas, and Mary Magdalene. When Jesus therefore saw his mother, and the disciple standing by, whom he loved, he saith unto his mother, Woman, behold thy son! Then saith he to the disciple, Behold thy mother! And from that hour that disciple took her unto his own home.

> John 19: 25–7

6. Hymn: When my love to God grows weak

1. When my love to God grows weak,
   When for deeper faith I seek,
   Then in thought I go to thee,
   Garden of Gethsemene.

2. There I walk amid the shades,
   While the lingering twilight fades;
   See that suffering, friendless one,
   Weeping, praying there alone.

3. When my will to love grows weak,
   When for stronger faith I seek,
   Hill of Calvary, I go
   To thy scenes of fear and woe.

4. There behold his agony,
   Suffered on the bitter tree;
   See his anguish, see his faith,
   Love triumphant still in death.

5. Then to life I turn again,
   Learning all the worth of pain,
   Learning all the might that lies
   In a full self-sacrifice.

6. And I praise with firmer faith
   Christ, who vanquished pain and death;
   And to Christ enthroned above
   Raise my song of selfless love.

J. R. Wreford and Samuel Longfellow

7. The Fourth Words

Now from the sixth hour there was darkness over all the land until the ninth hour. And about the ninth hour Jesus cried with a loud voice, saying, Eli, Eli, lama sabachthani? that is to say, My God, my God, why hast thou forsaken me?

Matthew 27: 45–6

8. Chorus (or solo): Drop, drop, slow tears

Drop, drop, slow tears,
And bathe those beauteous feet,
Which brought from heav'n
The news and Prince of Peace.

Cease not, wet eyes,
His mercies to entreat;
To cry for vengeance
Sin doth never cease.

In your deep floods
Drown all my faults and fears;
Nor let his eye
See sin, but through my tears.

Phineas Fletcher

9. Chorus/Hymn: Were you there?

1. Were you there when they crucified my Lord?
   Were you there when they crucified my Lord?
   Oh! Sometimes it causes me to tremble, tremble, tremble,
   Were you there when they crucified my Lord?

2. Were you there when they nailed him to the tree?

3. Were you there when they pierced him in the side?

4. Were you there when the sun refused to shine?

5. Were you there when they crucified my Lord?

American folk hymn

10. The Fifth Words

After this, Jesus knowing that all things were now accomplished, that the scripture might be fulfilled, saith, I thirst. Now there was set a vessel full of vinegar: and they filled a sponge with vinegar, and put it upon hyssop, and put it to his mouth.

John 19: 28–9

11. Chorus and solo/semichorus: Ave verum corpus

Ave verum corpus, natum de Maria Virgine;
Vere passum immolatum in cruce pro homine:
Cuius latus perforatum fluxit aqua et sanguine:
Esto nobis praegustatum in mortis examine.

Jesu, our redeemer, born of the Virgin Mary;
On the cross he suffered and was sacrificed for humankind.
For his side was pierced and flowed with water and holy blood:
Now his body feeds us in his death, for evermore.

Mediaeval Latin Hymn, English paraphrase A.B.

12. The Sixth Words

When Jesus therefore had received the vinegar, he said, It is finished.

John 19: 30

13. Arioso: God so loved the world

God so loved the world, that he gave his only begotten Son, that whosoever believeth in him should not perish, but have everlasting life. For God sent not his Son into the world to condemn the world; but that the world through him might be saved.

John 3: 16–17

14. The Seventh Words

Father, into thy hands I commend my spirit: and having said thus, he gave up the ghost.

Luke 23: 46

15. Chorus: In the departure of the Lord

In the departure of the Lord,
Of mortal body's vital breath,
There lies a mystery worth record,
Which he did show us here on earth:
That we, in life and death, each hour
Must follow Christ our Saviour.

Sir William Leighton

16. Hymn: When I survey the Wondrous Cross

1. When I survey the Wondrous Cross,
   On which the Prince of glory died,
   My richest gain I count but loss,
   And pour contempt on all my pride.

2. Forbid it, Lord, that I should boast,
   Save in the death of Christ my God;
   All the vain things that charm me most,
   I sacrifice them to his blood.

3. See from his head, his hands, his feet,
   Sorrow and love flow mingled down;
   Did e'er such love and sorrow meet,
   Or thorns compose so rich a crown?

4. Were the whole realm of nature mine,
   That were a present far too small;
   Love so amazing, so divine,
   Demands my soul, my life, my all.

Isaac Watts

Wondrous Cross

A meditation based on the traditional 'Seven Last Words' of Jesus Christ

ALAN BULLARD

1. Prelude

*Throughout the work, omit the sections in square brackets if strings are used.

This work may be accompanied either by organ or piano alone (using this score), or by string quartet, or string quintet/orchestra (2 vn, va, vc, db), together with organ or piano. A full score and set of string parts are available on sale or hire from the Publisher's Hire Library; the keyboard player uses this vocal score, omitting the sections in square brackets.

Printed in Great Britain

OXFORD UNIVERSITY PRESS, MUSIC DEPARTMENT, GREAT CLARENDON STREET, OXFORD OX2 6DP

2. The First Words

Luke 23: 33–4

Simply and freely
TUTTI or SOLO

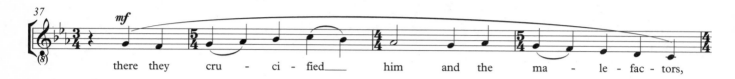

And when they were come to the place,— which is called— Cal - va - ry,

there they cru - ci - fied—— him and the ma - le - fac - tors,

one on the right hand, and the oth - er on the left. **Slower** Then said Je - sus,

Relaxed and calm ♩ = c.72

SOPRANOS
ALTOS
Fa- ther, for-give them, Fa- ther, for-give them, Fa- ther, for - give them, for-

TENORS
BASSES

Relaxed and calm ♩ = c.72

rit.
for they know not, for they know not what they do.

-give them, for - give them; for they know not, for they know— not what—— they do.

attacca

3. Hymn: There is a green hill far away

C. F. Alexander (1818–95) altd.

William Horsley (1774–1858)
accompaniment and descant Alan Bullard

*originally 'Without'

4. The Second Words

Luke 23: 39–43

Fast ♩. = c.58

f

101

MEN *(unis.)* or BASSES or SOLO

f *rhythmic and clear*

And one of the ma - le - fac - tors

108

f *f* *angry and mocking*

which were hanged railed on him, railed on him, say - ing, If thou be Christ,

116

ff *p*<*f* *ff*

if thou be Christ, if thou be Christ, Christ, save thy - self, save thy - self and us.

f

126

MEN *(unis.)* or TENORS or SOLO *f*

But the o - ther an - swer - ing re - buked him

5. The Third Words

John 19: 25–7

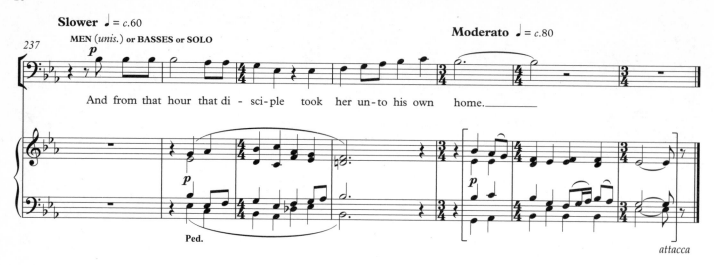

And from that hour that di - sci - ple took her un-to his own home.

6. Hymn: When my love to God grows weak

J. R. Wreford (1800–81) and Samuel Longfellow (1819–92)

Orlando Gibbons (1583–1625)
arranged and descant Alan Bullard

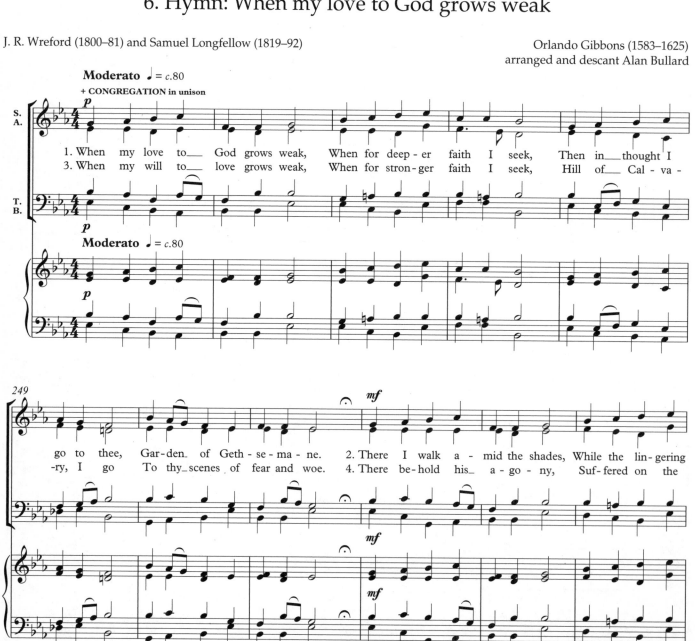

1. When my love to___ God grows weak, When for deep - er faith I seek, Then in___ thought I
3. When my will to___ love grows weak, When for stron - ger faith I seek, Hill of___ Cal - va -

go to thee, Gar - den___ of Geth - se - ma - ne. 2. There I walk a - mid the shades, While the lin - gering
-ry, I go To thy___ scenes of fear and woe. 4. There be - hold his___ a - go - ny, Suf - fered on the

twi - light fades; See that suf - fering, friend - less one, Weep - ing, pray - ing there a - lone.
bit - ter tree; See his an - guish, see his faith, Love tri - um - phant still in death.

5. Then to life I turn a - gain, Learn - ing all the worth of pain, Learn - ing all the might that lies

f

Piano RH: optional 8ve to end of hymn

SOPRANO DESCANT

ff

6. And I praise with fir - mer faith Christ, who van - quished

ALL OTHER VOICES

ff

6. And I praise with fir - mer faith Christ, who van - quished

In a full self - sa - cri - fice.

ff

pain and death; And to Christ en-throned a-bove Raise my song of self-less love.

pain and death; And to Christ en-throned a-bove Raise my song of self-less love.

7. The Fourth Words

Matthew 27: 45–6

Very slow ♩ = c.40

MEN (*unis.*) or SOLO
pp but rich

Now from the sixth hour there was dark - ness o-ver all the land un-til the ninth hour.

Dramatically ♩ = c.88

TUTTI (*unis.*) or SOLO *f*

And a-bout the ninth hour Je-sus cried with a loud voice, say - ing,

f sempre

S.
A.

E - li, E - li, la - ma sab-ach - tha - ni?

MEN (*unis.*) or SOLO
mf

T.
B.

f sempre

that is to say,

My God, my God,___ why hast thou for - sa - ken me, for - sa - ken me?___

16' (32')

8. Chorus (or solo): Drop, drop, slow tears

Phineas Fletcher (1582–1650)

NOTE: If necessary, this chorus may be accompanied, by strings when available, otherwise by organ or piano.
It may also be sung as a solo aria (soprano, or tenor 8ve lower) by singing the soprano line and using the instrumental accompaniment.

9. Chorus/Hymn: Were you there?

American folk hymn
arr. Alan Bullard

Note: Congregation sing (optionally) in verses 1 and 5 only, seated

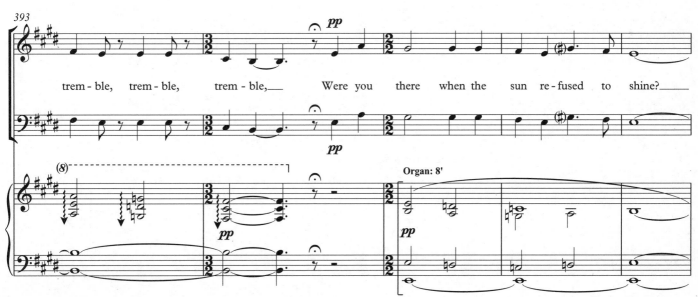

10. The Fifth Words

John 19: 28–9

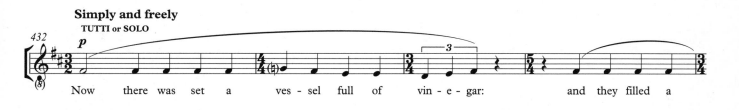

11. Chorus and solo/semi-chorus: Ave verum corpus

Mediaeval Latin Hymn
English paraphrase: A.B.

NOTE: this movement may also be sung as a solo aria (soprano, or tenor 8ve lower) by following these instructions:
1. After the first two bars, cut to bar 460, and sing Soprano line until bar 485
2. From bar 485, cut to bar 492, and sing Solo line
3. Bars 504–7, sing Soprano; bars 508–end, sing Solo

A modified version of this anthem, for SATB (without soloist) and organ/piano is available separately (ISBN 978-0-19-337999-2)

12. The Sixth Words

John 19: 30

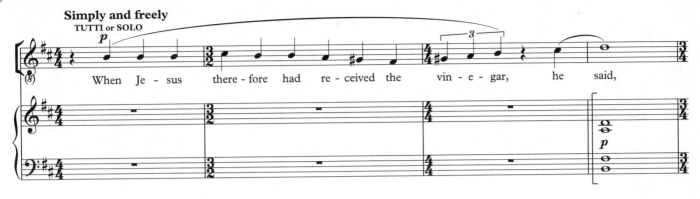

When Je - sus there - fore had re - ceived the vin - e - gar, he said,

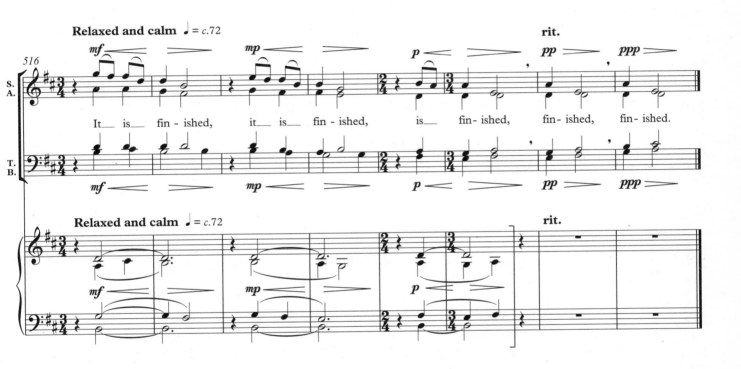

It__ is fin - ished, it__ is fin - ished, is__ fin - ished, fin - ished, fin - ished.

13. Arioso: God so loved the world

John 3: 16–17

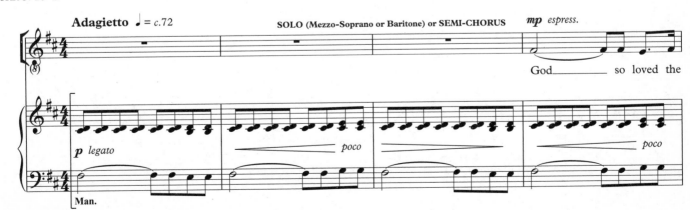

God_____ so loved the

14. The Seventh Words

Luke 23: 46

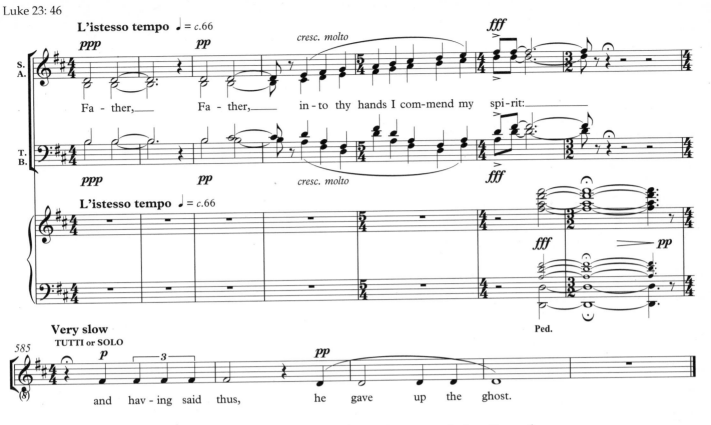

Fa - ther,___ Fa - ther,___ in - to thy hands I com-mend my spi - rit:

Very slow
TUTTI or SOLO

and hav - ing said thus, he gave up the ghost.

15. Chorus: In the departure of the Lord

Sir William Leighton (*c.*1560–1617)

In the de - par - ture of the Lord, Of mor - tal bo - dy's vi - tal breath,___ There lies a

mys - tery worth re - cord, Which he did show us here on earth:___ That we, in life and death, each

hour Must fol - low Christ our Sa - viour, must fol - low Christ our Sa - viour.

16. Hymn: When I survey the Wondrous Cross

Isaac Watts (1674–1748)

Edward Miller (1735–1807)
accompaniment and descant Alan Bullard

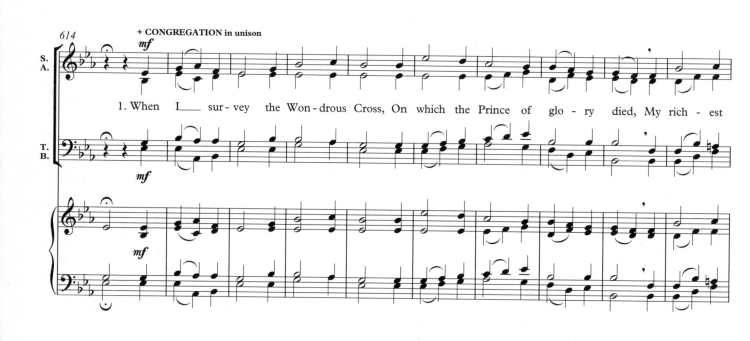

Easter 2011